T0065383

ALWAYS SAFE
Learn to win without fighting

TJ Johnston

authorHOUSE®

AuthorHouse™
1663 Liberty Drive
Bloomington, IN 47403
www.authorhouse.com
Phone: 833-262-8899

Cover photo credit:
Joey Ingalls

Interior photo credits:
Predator: Joey Ingalls, Ed Wolf, Johnny Gee, Nick Swanson
Criminal Entry: JB Johnston

Published by AuthorHouse 11/23/2020

ISBN: 978-1-6655-0577-2 (sc)
ISBN: 978-1-6655-0576-5 (e)

Print information available on the last page.

This book is printed on acid-free paper.

In memory of my friend and mentor Lt. Col Jeff Cooper.

Dedicated to my wife Madalyn who pushed me to finish this book.

CONTENTS

Foreword..ix

Introduction...xi

Chapter 1 Attackers..1

Chapter 2 The Cooper Color Codes of Awareness.........................6

Chapter 3 Always Safe in the Home.......................................36

Chapter 4 Always Safe - Conclusion......................................54

Home Security Checklist..61

FOREWORD

Another book on self-defense? Oh, come on…

No, this is a violence-AVOIDANCE *SYSTEM!*

By understanding the elements of fighting, we can avoid most situations that contribute to a violent altercation. We will explore what causes violence and how it escalates, and then set up a systematic approach to preventing those causes from getting out of control.

Anyone who has faced a life-threatening situation knows the feeling when fear takes over and the peculiar things that happen when the "red rage" is in charge. We need to put into place a system that will keep us away from that threshold and warn us when the dark clouds of confrontation gather on the horizon. As the police reports show in every city, there is violence around us every day. It takes more than luck to avoid it. We need to be proactive to prevent becoming a passive victim.

It's not difficult, but it takes a bit of the warrior mindset and an unshakeable belief that your life is worth defending. Sadly, as we pack more and more people into closer proximity and cause them to interact with greater frequency and intensity, learning to stay safe is becoming ever more critical.

"If a soldier's body is a gun, his hands and feet the bullets, then his mind is the trigger. Absence of the trigger renders the rest of the gun ineffective."

The Elite Forces Handbook of Unarmed Combat - Ron Shillingford, Thomas Dunne Books, St. Martin's Press; Copyright Amber Books Ltd 2000

INTRODUCTION

This is NOT another book on self-defense. This one is meant to PRECEDE all the others!

If you've perused your local bookstore, you've probably noticed that there are many books out there that will tell you how to cripple bad guys with exotic strikes or kick them into celibacy. Other books will tell you how to shoot/stab/or twist their heads till they come off. That's not the purpose of this book. This book is designed to keep you OUT OF THOSE SITUATIONS that require physical self-defense. And from my experience, it's easy to learn if you have a *system*.

My business is AllSafe Defense Systems. It's what I do for a living: teaching people how to live their lives without fear. Some students want to learn how to fight. Some want to learn how to shoot (I am an NRA

Training Counselor and train instructor candidates on teaching firearms and marksmanship). I encourage ALL of them to learn how to live *defensively*, so they will never have to fight or shoot. This book is that system.

I've been instructing self-defense since 1971. My sifu (teacher) thought you couldn't learn how to fight without actually *fighting*, meaning you had to hit another person and be hit by them to understand what happens in a fight. He was right.

For my contact students, I've adopted his methodology. In this contact environment, there are no rules, no prohibited targets, and no referee. There lurks the real danger of getting seriously hurt. That risk of danger does something to the human mind. I call it "tempering by fire."

But this book isn't about contact fighting. Fighting is ugly. It's brutal, bestial, painful, and terrifying. You won't really *know* adrenaline (up close and personal) until you have to fight for your life. But you can learn how to deal with the powerful effects of the "adrenaline dump" by practiced visualization and training.

There are all levels of training. The ultimate is to fight for a living. As any trained fighter will tell you, you learn something about yourself when you experience that out-of-body sensation as you watch your training kick in and have the pleasure to see that it works.

Few *NORMAL* people want to have this experience. They are the thrill-seekers who I call "adrenaline junkies." These warriors join Marine Recon units, the Navy SEALS, or the Army Special Forces and "be all they can be." Most of the rest of us will content ourselves with AVOIDING the terror of a life-and-death struggle. This book is designed for you.

This book is specially written for those people who are victims of fear. Like ground squirrels, they come out of their holes in the morning, furtively scurry around their daily existence, fearful that at any time, somebody will victimize them. Then they race home and barricade themselves behind a half dozen locks and hope and pray they will survive another long, dark, dreaded night.

Another concern is the Rambo-types, armed themselves to the teeth and looking for every opportunity to rid the gene pool of future pond scum. They are accidents waiting to happen. As civilized people, our goal should be to live full, happy, productive lives, uninterrupted by life-shattering violence. *This is a violence-avoidance book.*

I do have an underlying theme to this text: society must become more responsible for their personal safety. Avoidance is the first step. Deterrence is the next step. Those with the requisite aptitude and attitude should carry concealed weapons.

A life of crime should be hazardous. We can help each other live better by making the *CRIMINALS* afraid! I have a similar reason why EVERYBODY should learn CPR—so that someday when I have a heart attack, somebody nearby will have the capability to save *MY* life.

Likewise, we can work together to stop crime. We don't need more police. We certainly don't need to better arm and "militarize" our police. I am convinced that we can put most criminals out of business by adopting the simple systems advocated in this book.

Most criminals don't start as psychopaths. It's a learned behavior through repeated crimes. And as they continue to prey on people, they escalate. Each crime they commit, they become more aggressive, more violent, and more deadly.

We need to stop the juniors in training. Over time, criminals adopt the attitude that people are sheep, waiting to be harvested. We need to show them—by force if necessary—that it's easier (certainly less hazardous!) to get a job and pay taxes than rob people. If we deter them early in their development, we may turn them around before they become killers.

I have had the pleasure of learning from several "masters" who have shared their knowledge with me. Sadly, in the world of self-defense trainers, egos seem to rule. These lions of the combative arts seem to be competing with each other. In reality, they all have something really valuable to offer, but they seem to be segregated in their own kingdoms of mastery. I think it's time to bring their various training tips together into one comprehensive learning opportunity. Thus, this book is a unique presentation of the combined knowledge from several different sources of expertise.

I enjoyed serving on the NRA Board of Directors with Jeff Cooper, the founder of Gunsite, the Modern Pistol Technique, and the International Practical Shooting Confederation. During my terms, I recruited Jeff to join the Education and Training Committee to develop a better Personal Protection course. I have trained with Jeff and have spent many hours working with and corresponding with him over the years. Naturally, his perspective has had considerable influence on this book, but not as merely blind allegiance.

For example, I chose to use the Color Codes as established by Jeff Cooper instead of those advocated by Massad Ayoob. It was a deliberate choice: I think simpler is better. I'm bold enough to believe that Massad would agree, knowing that he emphasizes in his classes that, under the extreme stress of an urgent and life-threatening crisis, everything must be reduced to gross motor skills.

I have been rightfully accused of being a "minimalist" to boil down everything to the simplest, most basic ingredients. Specifically, in self-defense training, I think that is the best way to train. This book is designed to be as direct and straightforward as possible.

This is true in all of the fighting arts, from boxing to fencing, to shooting. If you watch the combatants in the Ultimate Fighting Championships, you will see competitors from all of the different martial arts coming together to beat each other into imbecility. You will see thundering knee lifts and crushing elbow strikes. But gone from their techniques are the spinning butterfly and tornado kicks. You won't see the winners using the dreaded axe kick or clever-looking "ridge hand" strikes. You WILL see extremely durable contact fighters throwing simple jabs and crosses, with an occasional hook or straight thrust kick. Indeed, it is better to boil down the soup's confusion to make a richer, more effective broth.

And so this book is a compilation and distillation of many different aspects of self-defense. It is mostly concerned with avoiding fighting, but the mindset required to *control* a fight is the best mindset necessary to *prevent* a fight. It is a kind of Zen attitude: to control a fight, you must first control yourself.

It is necessary to offer a disclaimer that this book will NOT GUARANTEE that you will never be caught in a violent situation if you follow every recommendation. Stuff happens, and sometimes life sucks. The systems offered in this book will minimize your victimization and greatly enhance your survivability if the dreaded situation occurs.

In this book's conclusion, I will editorialize because I'm motivated to write this book to encourage people to take charge of their lives. We must become less dependent on government institutions and the much-maligned law enforcement people to provide for our safety and well-being. If that sounds good to you, then please enjoy this presentation.

CHAPTER 1

ATTACKERS

Why do people attack other people?

We're nice people. We're "civilized." One of the most common responses to a violent attack is "Why ME!???" No one should ever want to hurt us. We try to be polite. We try to see other people when we change lanes on the freeway. We try not to make fun of the way they dress or their stupid kids. But for some reason, some people feel some need to harm us or take what we own.

We can list attackers by three different criteria. And this is important because it will determine how we respond to them, should they turn their aggression on us:

The three basic types of attackers include:

Enraged

Predators

Perceived threat (preemptive)

Most of us have witnessed the first one. We've seen people so angry they strike out at others. They have become so frustrated that they feel they have no other outlet for their energy but to attack. They may have a short fuse or be  struggling with unrestrained aggravation. They are Enraged.

The second reason is more sinister and can be much more dangerous. The second reason people attack other people is that they want to take something from us. The Predator wants your money, your car, your body, or your life.

There is a third reason why people will attack, and that is "Perceived Threat." Law enforcement has more significant concern with this attacker. For example, a criminal will attack cops when they are a "three-striker" or feel they have no other choice than resist arrest.

Unless you're a politician, we civilians will rarely have this problem. Since you're not arresting people regularly, the only way you'll confront this situation is if somebody considers you a threat and determines they have to harm you to relieve the threat. So if you don't hit on your neighbor's wife or husband, you won't have to face this kind of attacker. Even if you do and get caught, you'll most likely see them turn into the Enraged. If they're particularly nasty and plot your demise, they will follow all the Predator's same steps. They're just more dedicated.

What's the difference between the Enraged and the Predator?

The difference may be noticeable, but it is an important question. Your anticipation and your defense reaction to the two assailants will be different for each one. Both the Enraged and the Predator can be very aggressive. They both can be deadly dangerous. But the most significant most crucial difference between the two is *premeditation*.

The Enraged will blow up right there in front of you. Like a grenade: boom! If you aren't completely asleep, you will certainly see them coming. And in most situations, you will have time to react.

Your main objective with the Enraged will be to diffuse the situation. If you can keep it from escalating to violence, you will save a lot of stress and a lot of time in a courtroom.

The biggest problem with diffusing (or "verbal de-escalation") is to prevent your ego from getting involved. Many of us find our temperature rising when confronted by some butthead who is wildly out of control. It becomes a contest of profanity until the lower form of life becomes physically enraged. We will feel our own anger welling up from inside, being provoked by his irrational assault on you: the "nice guy." Then the situation can become dangerous. But we will deal with that later.

The Predator is like a cat, stalking its prey. In fact, after watching and reading many interviews with convicted criminals, it is apparent that many of these sociopaths view citizens as sheep.

Career criminals consider it their "job" to harvest the sheep, and if you're too incompetent to stop them, then, in their mind, you deserve to be mugged, raped, robbed, or murdered. These sharks go about their business virtually without malice and certainly without any feeling of concern or remorse for their damage to peaceable citizens' lives and mental health. You have something they want. According to their twisted reasoning, if you don't have the skills or resources to stop them, it's YOUR fault.

But these psychopaths aren't looking for a career challenge. They aren't crooks because they aspire to achieve. The majority of street hoods are looking for an easy mark. Their psyche can't afford for them to lose. They will do anything necessary to get what they want EXCEPT risk a likely chance of getting caught, injured, or killed.

Some thrill-seekers will enter a domicile, KNOWING that it's occupied. Law enforcement refers to this as a "hot prowl." These guys are really spooky because they don't fear getting caught, injured, or killed. They are confident they will succeed because these hoodlums unquestionably know they have the resources to prevail. They know they have more troops or are better armed than the homeowner. We'll deal with them later too.

The critical weakness to exploit in defeating the Predator is his premeditation: he has to see you first. But! If HE can see YOU, YOU can see HIM. If you see him, you can take actions to deter or stop his further advance.

But if you don't see him, just keep eating grass and hope that he picks someone else in the flock. Otherwise, you're about to become dinner for someone higher up the food chain.

The first and most crucial step of our self-defense system is to be AWARE.

CHAPTER 2

THE COOPER COLOR CODES OF AWARENESS

In his classes at Gunsight, Colonel Jeff Cooper taught that the mind is the weapon. Being armed with a firearm has little to do with the ability to defend oneself. To paraphrase one of my favorite analogies that he espoused:

> "Considering yourself armed by the mere possession of
> a firearm is like calling yourself a musician while sitting
> at a piano."

Until or unless the mind is trained to resist, a person is a *mark*, waiting to become a victim. The first part of that training is becoming aware. Another useful slogan:

> A good commander may be defeated, but he should never be surprised.

Anybody can be surprised. One of the essential tactics in fighting is to overwhelm your opponent with too many things to consider and deluge him with sensory overload. The surprise is the best tool to accomplish this. While his mind is sorting out the real from the feints, we can press the attack with minimal danger.

So our first problem in our self-defense system is to avoid being taken by surprise. The simple remedy: stay aware.

Colonel Cooper devised a simple yet effective system of categorizing the different stages of awareness. He assigned colors to make it easy to remember. The first color is white.

Condition White

In their course "Personal Protection in the Home," the NRA identifies this first level as "unaware" and, in a word, that pretty well sums it up. But this is not a negative state. It's not like being inane stupid or blind drunk. It is a positive state where we don't have to be afraid. It should be of paramount importance to establish an environment to find a secure refuge where we can go "white."

Ideally, our homes should be that refuge. That doesn't mean we lock an argumentative family member outdoors. (That's a different book.) Instead, we should install the necessary security devices so we can sleep, read a book,

People on cell phones are usually in condition white.

watch TV, or mess around with our lovers without worrying about our safety. What is essential is to set up our home environment so that an intruder will be forced to give us some significant warning to take us to Condition Yellow. We'll spend considerable energy on this in Chapter 3.

Condition Yellow

Here's how to stay in "Yellow" while on your phone.

Once we leave the security of our homes, we must learn to live in Condition Yellow. The NRA has titled this state merely as "aware." The state of being aware is not a stressful or paranoid state of worry or fear. Instead, it is like a game of talking to yourself and continuously sizing up the situation around you.

Colonel Cooper recommends developing your awareness by actually making it a game where you keep track of how well you pay attention. If anyone enters your personal space or passes you on the highway, and you didn't see them coming, you give yourself a demerit. At the end of the week or month, you total up your demerits and deprive yourself of a usual treat—either a dessert or drink. As the Colonel suggests, you'll either wind up thinner or more sober. Not a dire punishment!

The goal of the exercise is to make you see what's going on around you. Notice people. See how they relate to you. *Most importantly, notice people who are noticing you.*

Bad guys set up their marks. They look at and evaluate prospective targets. If they think you've seen them and noted them, chances are they'll be looking for another potential victim.

It is crucial to identify in your mind anyone you view as suspicious or threatening. Make it a conscious mental note. Talk to yourself (ideally without others hearing!). If you see someone following you through the Mall, or notice someone watching you walk from your car to your work, take a good look at him. Describe them to yourself. Note them well enough to be able to pick them out of a line-up.

Make it a game to be able to satisfy a police investigation by noting their race, approximate height, and weight. Since most of us aren't used to estimating height and weight, use your own statistics, and compare. How much bigger and heavier is the potential threat? Are they fatter or thinner, muscular or flabby? Notice their hair color, cut, or lack of hair. Facial hair? How about their clothing: what color is it? Are they wearing designer tennis shoes? Does their clothing have trademark names? Be especially mindful of any distinguishing marks or tattoos. If they talk, notice any ethnic slang or accents in their speech that will help you identify their heritage. Try to find any adjectives that you can apply.

It is a comment on society's sad state that you may incur gang members' wrath who think you are "dissing" them by staring at them. Perhaps in that situation, you may choose to look secretly at them. But make mental notes. And be sure *they know* you see them.

Keep your antennae tuned. Note anything that you don't "feel" is quite right. Your intuition is very reliable. For example, in the morning, when you're leaving for work, if you see a couple of guys sitting in a car parked outside your home, don't ignore them. Get out of your car, go up behind them and jot down their license number. Or better still, take out a camera, go to the side window, and photograph them.

If they are innocent, you may establish some new and entertaining relationships. If they are parked there for no good reason, chances are they'll be leaving in a hurry. Either way, if you come home to find your residence burgled, you can hand the police some hard evidence to aid in their investigation.

While moving through public places, most experienced martial artists make a pastime of noting individuals who look like possible problems. It isn't challenging to identify guys who look physically tough, who have "wolf eyes" that have seen violence and are not intimidated by it. They may look like Sasquatch with animal-like hair everywhere, or they may be a skinhead with "tatts" all over. Or they may be clean-cut and buffed, with that predatory look in their eyes, and they move like a cat.

It may seem strange to those uninitiated into the fighting arts, but trained people evaluate *everyone* as potential assailants even though the other person isn't paying particular attention to anyone at all. As one of Murphy's Laws of Interpersonal Combat states: be polite to everyone but be prepared to kill them.

The purpose of this drill is to make you see people BEFORE they see you. That way, you won't have to give up your chocolate at the end of the month. More importantly, it will help assure that you won't be surprised by your assailant.

Condition Orange

When you see someone watching you, notice him following you, or tailing your car, you go to Condition Orange. For this condition, the NRA's term is "alert," like a hunting dog "alerts" on a bird. There is a better word: *unease*. Something isn't quite right. Your gut is quietly talking to you, and you're not comfortable with what it's saying.

Condition Orange is when you are aware of a **specific potential threat**. At this point, you're not under attack, but it could be imminent. Some examples would include subtle things like:

> You see the car behind you, making the same turn with you for the third time.
> The guy you noticed following you in the Mall is now hanging around near your car.
> You see a gang of kids sitting on the hood of your car in the parking lot.

Or it could be something dramatic like:

> Your home alarm is blaring at two o'clock in the morning.
> Coming home from work, you find the door to your apartment unlocked and open.
> You see a gang of toughs crossing the street to YOUR side.

Each of these situations demands your response. What should you do?

You need to establish an **Immediate Action Plan**. The NRA lists five possible responses to an attack. This list needs a little work.

First, we don't want to consider them as a *list of possible responses*. That makes them seem like chance knee-jerk reactions. Instead, it's better to be proactive and make them *choices*. The NRA's list includes: fight, flight, freeze, posture, and submit. To improve this, just a little bit, remove "freeze" and insert "diffuse." We'll explore this in greater depth shortly.

But first, let's take a short detour. We'll come back to this point after we establish a few concepts of fighting.

Which is faster: action or reaction?

Many people guess "reaction" because they think of it as a mindless knee-jerk response to some stimulus. But this is wrong. As Webster's defines it, reaction is "a response to a stimulus." In other words, the stimulus occurs; the mind perceives the stimulus and causes the body to respond. This time of synapse response can mean the difference between life and death in a violent confrontation. And this is especially true if the "mindless, knee-jerk response" is wrong.

We are calling our plan an "Immediate *ACTION* Plan" because *action is faster than reaction*. Because action starts first, it has a more significant advantage. Bad guys set traps and prefer to ambush their prey because they know the element of surprise will often debilitate their targets. It takes time for the victim to realize they are under attack. It takes additional time to decide when or whether to resist. And it takes time to determine HOW to respond. Each step of this discovery takes valuable, life-threatening time. As Rory Miller states in his excellent book *Facing Violence*, time is damage.

To teach his fighter pilots dogfighting, Air Force Colonel John Boyd developed a practical concept designed to be the foundation of rational thinking in confusing or chaotic situations. He called it the OODA Loop. The four steps are to Observe, Orient, Decide Act. These are repeated again and again until a conflict finishes. Our goal is to speed up and shorten our Loop and cause our adversary to get behind or lost in his OODA Loop.

To resist an attack, you can't afford to be taken by surprise. Your Condition Yellow training will hopefully prevent that. But as you see the confrontation about to occur, you need to make pro-active choices. So let's explore our filtered list.

Choices When Confronted

1. **FIGHT**: no definition required here. All that is needed is the proper mindset. Once you have chosen to resist, you must think first and foremost: *NEVER GIVE UP*. Make up your mind that your adversary will have to destroy you to prevail over you.

This mindset will make you indomitable and give you strength and conviction far beyond your usual "civilized" capacity. It will make merciless in your opposition, especially when you counterattack. Often against common thugs, this fearlessness will engender fear in your adversary, and the chances are good that they will break off their attack, hide tail and run away. Criminals aren't looking for a career challenge.

2. **FLIGHT**: if you have the opportunity to avoid a confrontation, take it. Sanford Strong, a former police officer from San Diego, has

written an excellent book entitled "Strong On Defense" [Pocket Books – Simon & Schuster]. In his book, Strong insists that this should be your most important goal. Everything you do from the first instance of contact should be designed to get away as quickly as possible. Don't let ego cause you to stand your ground and duke it out. Even if you win, you will probably pay the price, sometimes financial, often painful.

As Heavyweight Thug Mike Tyson demonstrated in one of his out-of-the-ring altercations, striking the human jaw with a closed fist will often break the hand. The goal in dealing with a confrontation is to prevail, ideally at the least possible cost. And if you can avoid the fight, you won't pay anything. At least not for the moment.

Something even more insidious: even if you are entirely innocent and provoked into a defensive dispute if you injure your adversary due to defending yourself, you could find yourself in court defending your actions. The net result will require you to hire a criminal or civil defense lawyer to *PROVE* your innocence, and that process can be costly. As you must know and accept, in our court system, you get all the justice you can afford. As the OJ Trial of the Century proved, in a courtroom, *anything* can happen.

3. **DIFFUSE**: law enforcement uses this technique every day. It is beneficial when dealing with the enraged attacker (any attempt to diffuse the predator will not be successful). Diffusing the situation is a skill that is overlooked in many self-defense courses but can serve to prevent an altercation from escalating to a violent level.

The clinical field calls this technique "verbal de-escalation." They use it to treat aggressive patients. We can employ the same system when facing someone angry or frustrated and wants to take out their rage on us.

The two components of our system of verbal de-escalation are *listening* and *reasoning.*

Listening is a skill we can practice daily. The goal is to listen *actively* and *empathetically.* Don't interrupt, argue, or try to convince. Want to see a kid throw a tantrum? Just keep saying, "no." Instead, allow full expression of needs and grievances when appropriate. You will need to listen with interest and concern and then validate feelings.

Interrupting or denying feelings tends to escalate the anger. When the person pauses, calmly say something like, "I understand you are upset." Remain nonjudgmental at this point until you can obtain more information and you can address the problem.

Show empathy for the person's feelings but not for his or her hostile and abusive behavior (e.g., "I understand that you have a right to feel angry, but it is *not* okay for you to threaten me.").

Set limits firmly and explain the consequences without threats or anger toward their inappropriate behavior. Use an authoritative but respectful tone (e.g., "Please sir, STOP. If you continue to threaten and show hostility, this conversation is over, and you will force me to… [implement your *back up* Immediate Action Plan].").

Provide choices where possible in which both alternatives are safe ones (e.g., "Would you like to continue discussing this calmly here or would you prefer to go get a cup of coffee?").

Use a tone of voice that is calming. Avoid tones that suggest impatience, disgust, or sarcasm. Volume should be moderate—not too loud or too soft. Speak clearly and slowly. Too rapid or halting speech conveys agitation and loss of control.

Clear up misunderstandings and respond to valid complaints. Respond selectively; only answer informational questions (e.g., "Why is that space yours?"), not abusive ones. The example is a real information-seeking question. Answer this type of problem respectfully. Do not answer rude or offensive questions (e.g., "How did you get so freakin' ugly?"). Do not respond directly to questions like those. Instead, divert the conversation at this point.

Trust your instincts. If you feel that verbal de-escalation is not working, stop, and get a safe distance away from the hostile person and be prepared to escape or take physical control of the situation.

Maintain a distance of at least two arms' lengths between you and your aggressor. This distance will allow you reaction time from attacks such as grabs, strikes, and lunges.

Angle your body about 45 degrees to the individual's "power line." The power line is the straight line from your opponent's center to your center. This stance not only reduces your target size in the event of an attack but also prepares you to escape when necessary. It also shields the more vulnerable parts of your body with less sensitive parts.

Place your hands in front of your chest in an open and relaxed position. This gesture appears non-threatening and positions your hands for blocking and counterattacking if the need arises.

Avoid crossed arms, hands in the pocket, or arms behind the back since it not only puts you at a tactical disadvantage, but many people interpret this as negative body language.

If possible, casually position yourself behind a barrier such as a sofa, desk, large chair, counter, table, or other large objects when possible.

Reasoning is less "logical rebuttal" and more a manner of speaking. 65% of our communication is non-verbal. It is imperative to be able to identify what we are communicating non-verbally. There are three speaking elements that we must control and use to maximize our effectiveness: pitch, inflection, and volume.

Pitch refers to the frequency and range of your voice. In stressful circumstances, our voice tends to rise to a higher register, sometimes becoming shrill. Speakers using a lower pitch are more likely to be perceived as telling the truth and being able to stand behind their words. In light of this, to present an assertive de-escalating message, keep your voice as steady as possible and at its lowest natural pitch. Speaking slowly with a measure cadence under stress takes practice!

Inflection refers to the variations in the voice's pitch while speaking. For assertive power, it's best to keep a level intonation. Many people sabotage their communication power by ending statements on a rising inflection, which causes strong statements to sound weak as if asking a question. Consider saying, "I want you to leave now," with all the words at the same pitch. Now, try saying it with the last word in a high pitch.

When the "now" sounds like a question, even a polite listener may be confused about what you want.

Volume is the loudness of your voice. In de-escalation, you do not necessarily want to yell or shout. Verbal de-escalations are most effective when the speaker uses a calm, firm voice.

It depends mainly on the specific situation, but in many circumstances, the best approach is to speak in a firm, calm, clear voice with a smooth tone and a strong sense of conviction behind your words. This demeanor may get your point across without triggering the aggressor into a more agitated or violent state.

If you choose to raise the volume, be sure to maintain a steady level pitch. Carefully observe the response you get. If the other person's agitation increases when you increase the volume, lower it, and keep adjusting as needed, to remain in control and safely give yourself the best chance to diffuse the confrontation.

Most importantly, when attempting to diffuse, remain calm and in control. Breathe naturally to help control your emotional response. Do not become verbally defensive. When someone is challenging or yelling at you, the natural but incorrect tendency is to respond likewise. Unfortunately, a defensive response tends to cause the other person to become even angrier. A calm reply and a cool head are essential.

4. **POSTURE**: The NRA defines this as "combat without contact," which captures the essence pretty well. Like in the animal kingdom, you will have to puff up your feathers and stand up on your hind legs to look threatening enough to deter further aggression. Cops call it "command presence." If you have the size and voice, or a badge and a radio car, it can be very successful.

Your "will" to never give up can be a valuable deterrent at this point. Showing this virulently stubborn will and refusing to be intimidated by the situation will give pause to many less-determined adversaries looking for an easy score. He thought he would scare you into compliance, and all he sees in response is teeth and claws.

If you don't have big teeth and claws, you'll need many small friends or an intimidating weapon.

It is important to note that posturing is NOT bluffing. If you aren't determined to overwhelm your adversary in a fighting confrontation, posturing may not be the best choice. To quote Mark Twain with a phrase popularized by former US Presidents Truman and Eisenhower:

"It isn't the size of the dog in the fight. It's the size of the fight in the dog."

Another important note: brandishing or displaying a firearm in hopes of deterring a criminal assault may be an effective form of posturing but can also lead to criminal prosecution. Most law enforcement agencies agree that a firearm's presentation can only occur where there are no other alternatives to stop a physically dangerous attack. This is the only time you can lawfully present a gun. You are not entitled to resolve a "threat" with lethal force. "He said he was going to kill me, so I shot him…" Sorry, chum. Only governments can use preemptive strikes. You're going to jail.

We'll revisit this discussion for our highest level of awareness: Red

5. **SUBMIT**: This seems to be something NO ONE considers a choice, but it is. And it doesn't mean that you give up and *surrender*.

The NRA's Refuse To Be A Victim program has an excellent suggestion when confronted by a robber. A crook sticks a gun in your face and growls, "Give me your money." You offer him a throw-away wallet where you show him a few singles and some expired credit cards. When he reaches for it, you "accidentally" drop it and run as fast as you can. The adrenaline rush will help make good your escape. (As any experienced handgunner will admit, hitting a laterally moving target is quite difficult!). You haven't given him anything of value and have stopped a potentially lethal force situation from escalating.

It is important to note that "giving up" is not advisable. Don't surrender and become compliant, thinking the bad guy will treat you kindly if you don't make him mad. In his book, *Strong on Defense: Survival Rules to Protect You and Your Family from Crime,* Sanford Strong repeatedly emphasizes that the criminal will only become MORE savage and more emboldened by your compliance. If you're going to resist, you must resist *IMMEDIATELY* without hesitation or reservation.

Strong also makes a critical strategic point in his book. He underscores the crucial importance of never allowing the perpetrator to take you to a second location. It will only get worse when he has you alone and isolated in HIS environment.

FBI Statistics support the conclusion that if people fail to resist, they suffer more harm than those who fight back. To paraphrase a wonderful colloquialism from Neal Knox (shooter, gun writer, founder Firearms Coalition): you don't chase away a stray dog by giving him a bone. Strong documents in his book, on several occasions, compliant individuals accommodated their own torture and death.

In other words, a better choice is *not waiting to resist.* But if you choose the alternative to submit, *it is NOT giving up.* Your mind is already set on resisting, and submitting at this point is a *tactical* submission. *It is a ruse to gain a more significant advantage.*

There have to be limits preset in your mind, including when the perpetrator attempts to tie you up or take you to another location. When this happens, you can't wait for a "better" moment. You must resist without hesitation and, using every bit of the super-power given you by the adrenaline dump, attack with every bit of rage, strength, and violence you possess. You must remember the "warrior mindset": NEVER GIVE UP.

And so, when you first perceive a **Specific Potential Threat**, make an **Immediate Action Plan** from a deliberative choice of one of these five alternatives: fight, flight, diffuse, posture, or submit. Do this right away while your brain is still yours. While you are still rational *BEFORE,* the altercation starts: evaluate the situation. Make a logical decision and then decide on the final element in the Orange stage of awareness: a triggering event.

Triggering Event

Decide on a specific time to initiate your Immediate Action Plan. Draw a "line in the sand" that isn't apparent to your adversary. Once you set your plan in motion, you now become ACTIVE and force your adversary to become REACTIVE. You're now in charge of the confrontation. If you've made good choices, chances are the bad guy will immediately break off the attack. He's not interested in competing when it looks like he is going to lose. By definition, he's a coward, and most crooks can't stomach the idea of being bigger losers.

By doing all the prep work of coming up with an Immediate Action Plan and establishing your Triggering Event, you've made all your decisions. Once the "line" is crossed, you don't have to think. Because once "the balloon goes up," and the altercation begins, you won't have time to think or decide. Even more troubling, you won't have the ABILITY to think or make decisions.

Effect Of Adrenaline

In physiological terms, what happens to the individual when suddenly confronted with a life-and-death altercation?

Just above the kidneys are the adrenal glands, which secrete a powerful drug directly into the bloodstream. In his presentation "The Bulletproof Mind" (Calibre Press Audio), Lt. Colonel Dave Grossman includes a session entitled "How the Body Responds to Combat." In that session, he relates how the rush of adrenaline affects the human being.

It's common knowledge that adrenaline will cause tunnel vision, time dilation, and auditory exclusion. Let's explore these briefly:

Tunnel vision: While interviewing a robbery victim, a police officer asked the victim to describe her assailant. Her bewildered reply was, "It was a gun…with feet!"

Tunnel vision is whereby the source of the threat captures your focus. This narrowed field of view is the body's primal response to maintain absolute focus on the danger at hand. But this can be even more dangerous when there are multiple assailants.

At Front Sight, a shooting school near Pahrump, Nevada, Dr. Ignatius Piazza teaches his students to reflexively turn the head left then right after engaging a gunfight target to break the tunnel vision. Then he has his students visually verify the effectiveness of their hits. We need to be aware that our brains will keep our eyes focused on the greatest perceived danger, even to exclude other more serious threats. As the attack commences, look around. As they said in Viet Nam: "When in sh*t, check your six."

Time dilation: We've all heard stories about how, during a high-stress situation, everything seems to slow down. As Colonel Grossman points out, this is not a problem as long as you accept this fact and don't get mentally concerned with it. The brain is on hyper-speed with adrenaline and processing information much more rapidly. And although the body is still moving quickly, the brain is moving faster. It would be a real problem if you let doubt or insecurity about your ability to prevail creep into your thinking because you don't think you're moving fast enough. Don't be distracted by the sensation, and it won't be a problem.

Auditory exclusion: The rules at most firing ranges require that everyone wear hearing protection due to the potential hearing damage caused by the high decibel sound of gunfire. And yet some police officers have been involved in shootings where they weren't aware of the sound at all and suffered no ringing ears after the altercation. This is auditory exclusion. The primal brain discards the information that it doesn't value as necessary for surviving the next few seconds.

What is important to note is that your adversary is probably experiencing the same adrenaline rush as you are. And so when you point your .357 at him and calmly ask him to drop the knife, he may not even hear you. He's not ignoring you; he's just looking a gun with feet! Any commands you issue to your adversary must be powerfully shouted.

In his book, Colonel Grossman does an outstanding job relating to the effect of adrenaline on the heart and, in turn, how this accelerated heart rate affects the whole being. As the heartbeat increases beyond a specific rate, critical faculties begin to shut down.

In most healthy adults, you have a resting heart rate between 60-80 beats per minute. When the adrenaline dump occurs, that rate instantly shoots up to 150-200 beats per minute. Colonel Grossman breaks it out in this way:

115-145 beats per minute: vaso-constriction

> This sets your body at its optimal combat performance level. The blood to the extremities is reduced and supplied mainly to the large muscle groups such as the biceps, triceps, quads, and hamstrings. This fills the major muscles with oxygen-rich blood, giving them maximum explosive power. Because there is less blood flow to the extremities, any wounds sustained will have

minimal blood loss. And because of the lessened blood flow to the hands and fingers, there is a resultant loss in fine-motor skills. Manipulating a weapon will become much more difficult as if you were wearing boxing gloves or heavy mittens.

145-175 beats per minute:

At this point, the adrenaline becomes a detriment. When your heart rate gets to this speed, your complex motor skills fail. Only gross motor skills can be achieved. Your hands will only be useful as blunt clubs, incapable of any dexterity.

Above 175 beats per minute:

At this point, the fore-brain shuts down. You will no longer be capable of rational thought or discernment. The mid-brain is only capable of implementing the "fight or flight" mentality. Only the basic instincts of survival will be available.

According to Grossman, some extraordinary heart rates have been documented. They have recorded sustained heart rates of 200 beats per minute, with spikes up to 300 beats per minute. When you get over 200 beats per minute, the conscious brain is no longer in control. Paralysis begins to set it. You will *FREEZE*.

The key to surviving a violent encounter is to act *BEFORE* your heart rate reaches jackhammer speed. You know that sensory overload will occur if you aren't prepared. If you haven't pre-made your decision to act, you will have too many things to think about and too little time to decide. Even worse, you won't have confidence in making your decision. And worse still, as the adrenaline sets your heart racing, you won't have the ability to USE your brain to MAKE a decision. *FREEZE becomes the default if you don't set up your Immediate Action Plan while in Condition Orange.*

Colonel Grossman adds some excellent breathing tips to help control the runaway heart rate. For people who train to fight, this control is essential. But for our purposes, we need to understand and accept that the logical functioning brain will not be available once the altercation has begun. To repeat: any decisions that need to be made *MUST BE MADE WHILE IN CONDITION ORANGE.*

Now let's summarize our Condition Orange:

When a **Specific Potential Threat** confronts you, you must decide on an **Immediate Action Plan** by choosing one of five options:

> Fight
>
> Flight
>
> Diffuse
>
> Posture
>
> Submit

Evaluating the environment and the available options, you then need to establish the **Triggering Event**. Now your decisions have been made; you stand ready to deal with the situation. The rest is a matter of your tools and how well you've trained yourself to use them. Because once the Triggering Event has occurred, now we go to Condition Red.

Condition Red

The NRA terms this "alarm," which is kind of lame. Better title: *ACT!* You aggressively and without hesitation implement your Immediate Action Plan. Acknowledge that you are no longer thinking and rational. If you've chosen flight, you run like the wind.

If you've chosen to fight, then you must act without hesitation. Note that your first action will be the most critical and decisive. Statistically, most violent confrontations are concluded in a matter of seconds. Your adversary must be instantly surprised by your resistance's sheer intensity and violence, as Cooper wrote: violence trumps technique.

Every combat trainer will emphasize the same point. The *MIND IS THE WEAPON.* The firearm, knife, club, or fist is only a tool. And the tool is only as useful as the mind. Therefore the mindset is the essential aspect of controlling a violent altercation.

As stated before, the mindset has to be secure in the commitment not just to survive but to win. Even if you've chosen to fight, Strong suggests in his book that the mind should focus on the goal of fighting: to *ESCAPE*, not to subdue. Keeping this goal in mind is valuable if you're not defending your children or loved ones.

Regardless, you must be mentally prepared to prevail and will not accept failure. The thought of failure must be rejected from your mind. You become a beast designed for fighting, and there is no other consideration or concern. Any injury you sustain is unimportant. You are indomitable. You are the only possible victor, and there is no other alternative.

A person with this determination is really scary. And the bad guy facing you will be forced to appreciate that. Intimidation is one of his best tools, and when that doesn't work, he's a little short on alternatives.

Statistically, most violent encounters are over in a matter of seconds. All you have to do is stay alive and stay aggressive for that short time. With this mindset, you will prevail.

Escalating through the states of Awareness

It is virtually impossible to go from White to Red with any kind of effectiveness. The more you train for crisis response, the more quickly you will transition from Yellow to Red. But when you're in White, your mind is dormant and is unprepared to make the vital decisions necessary to meet and overcome a dangerous adversary.

As we stated before, your adversary must not surprise you. On the street, you maintain your awareness by looking around and noting who is watching you. But how do you sustain that awareness in your home?

Most of us can't afford armed patrols and surveillance cameras around our homes. So bad guys could be tramping through our flower beds and peeking in our windows. Worse still, they could be prying at our doors and windows, attempting to get at us while we sleep. What can we do?

There are many precautions we can take to ensure that our home is set up to relax and enjoy your life in Condition White. It would be best to take these measures to be confident that you have the necessary system to give you the warning essential to make that first step up the ladder.

CHAPTER 3

ALWAYS SAFE IN THE HOME

So how do we prepare our home to assure that we can live in Condition White? Our ultimate goal is to live without fear. Once again, we can develop a *defense system* to alleviate fear and let us rest without worry.

The system intends to "harden the target" and discourage the less-determined intruder. We can systematically scrutinize our home as a series of "perimeters." We can tighten and secure each perimeter depending on our neighborhoods, economics, and perceived threat level.

First Perimeter: What surrounds your home? Do you have a front or backyard? Do you live in an apartment or condominium complex with a shared yard? Do you live in a brownstone walk-up with noisy neighbors everywhere around you?

The most important question to ask about the curtilage around your domicile is, "Where can bad guys hide?" If it's *your* property, remove the hiding places. Put lights or structures to eliminate them. Or plant "unfriendly" vegetation like cactus or thorny bushes like holly or roses in those places.

If you can't change the landscape, modify your movement patterns to prevent being ambushed. Walk wide around corners to reveal any gremlins before you get within arms reach.

Elevators are traps. You have very few alternatives if you're inside an elevator with an aggressive assailant. If your perceived threat level is such that you usually don't fear to take the elevator, then enjoy the convenience. But should you notice someone on or near the elevator who gives you that "feeling," go to Condition Orange and take the stairs instead—you can always use the exercise! If he follows you, then start making your plan to go to Condition Red.

If practical, stay away from secluded places entirely or approach them fully aware and ready for what lurks there.

Second Perimeter: the exterior of your home. Can you lock yourself out? Some bad guys make a career out of "B&E"— breaking and entering. They will know all the

Use drapes or curtains to prevent people from seeing what is inside your home.

hiding places for your keys and your "secret" way to credit-card your door or slip a window.

You need to secure your home so that you would have to *break* something to get in. The system requires that we have a method of securing our domicile exterior to the degree that someone who is experienced at forcing doors, windows, and locks will have to break something or set off some alarm. This will bring us to our next level of awareness, either Yellow or Orange.

Any time you move into a rental unit, insist on re-keying the locks. And while you're at it, insist that a heavy-throw deadbolt be installed if there isn't one already. Don't ever trust your life on a little brass chain lock.

Most exterior front doors are solid, even on the least expensive apartments. Where you'll find easy access are the exterior doors on the sides or backdoors. These are usually flimsy hollow-core doors that any healthy Neanderthal could "shoulder." These need to be replaced with solid core doors.

Another type of door that makes silent entry possible are decorative glass doors, or doors within arms reach of windows. Glasscutters are quiet, available, and easy to use. Once that glass has been holed, the bad guy can reach in and unlock the door. Oops. Now we have a significant problem: he's inside, and *you don't know it*. Surprise: major league oops.

Third perimeter: The next system you need is some device that will alert you if your exterior perimeter is breached. There are many alarm systems available. There are new electronic sensors that indicate when a window or door is opened. These have replaced the older electric tape alarms that can be defeated by tinfoil. Interior motion sensors that can be attached to lights or sirens can assure that we effectively rouse from our beloved Condition White. Naturally, a motion sensor will have to be adjusted to identify adults from pets. As we all know, the ubiquitous car alarms—repeated false alarms will soon be ignored as if there were no alarms.

Another sound interior alarm is a dog. What we need is a good family pet that is bonded to us. We don't need a Doberman or pitbull that will get Maced by our letter carrier and eat the neighborhood school kids. We need a good (calm!) breed that will sound the alarm should there be something amiss.

It is best to have an INDOOR pet that will bark at the intruder and sound the alarm and identify where the problem is! Most times, burglars will avoid domiciles with dogs because of that attribute.

But suppose you have a problem with pets such as recalcitrant landlords or personal restrictions such as allergies. In that case, it may be possible to capitalize on the bad guy's concern with canines by displaying a "Beware of Dog" sign on the back gate. The bad guy isn't going to sue for false advertising. You can enhance the effect by placing a large dog food bowl or water bowl outside. Add a gnarly chewed-up "chew toy" for added emphasis on the destructive potential of the canines. How you get it already chewed up is your problem.

The fourth and last perimeter is your Safe Room. This is where you "make your stand." If you're facing someone who has defeated all your other perimeters and is still intent on getting to you, you're dealing with a very determined adversary.

Them versus Us

Let's consider the assets available to a resident and compare them to the intruder's assets.

INTRUDER:

1. <u>Element of surprise</u>

   The bad guy counts on this as his primary tactic. He hopes you are sleeping and content in your Condition White so he can take advantage of your inattention.

2. <u>Known resources</u>

   He knows if he's alone or has ten friends with him. You don't know what he has in terms of reinforcements, weapons, and backup.

3. <u>Known intent</u>

   He knows what he wants and what he will do to get it. You don't know if he wants your jewelry and CD collection or if he wants YOU.

4. Armed

He knows if he's armed or not--you don't. Statistically, intruders on a "hot prowl" are armed and ready to shoot anything threatening him. He knows anybody walking in is a potential target, and discerning no-shoot innocents doesn't constrain him. He will be faster to shoot because he doesn't have to decide about pulling the trigger.

RESIDENT:

1. Knowledge of the layout

The resident has intimate knowledge, not only of the kitchen and bathroom location but also of the sounds that emanate from the various rooms. The resident will know when he hears a particular door or drawer open or hears a creak on the staircase. If lights can be controlled from a master bedroom, there are more controls over the layout to gain an advantage over the intruder.

2. Ability to call for help

Bad guys can't call for the police. Within a reasonable period, there will be more guns waiting outside your home than any bad guy can counteract. The good guys can muster an army of remarkable capacity. All that is required is enough time, and the bad guys know that.

3. Armed?

    This is an individual choice, and it isn't an advantage OVER, the bad guy. It merely neutralizes him. A firearm only enhances the power of the holder. It's not a magic talisman. The adage of scaring an intruder away by racking the pump-action shotgun does have some merit. Most importantly, it tells the intruder that the resident is aware and ready to resist.

The intruder has a significant tactical advantage over the resident by surveying our list. And the resident surrenders his main asset when he hauls out his trusty rusty.38 or prized fowling gun and begins stumbling through the darkened house, asking, "Is anybody there?"

Military doctrine has proven that a smaller force can hold a fortified position against much superior numbers in warfare. Likewise, in-home defense, a fortified safe room can be impregnable by even a *gang* of bad guys. And by keeping them at bay for some time, you discourage their commitment. They know the homeowner can call for help and that the cavalry will soon arrive.

So how do we fortify your safe room?

The NRA's Personal Protection in the Home course does an admirable job of detailing an excellent safe room's best qualities. Let's take their suggestions and embellish them.

Firstly, it should have only one doorway. Every trained combatant understands a "choke point" where resources must be funneled through a constriction. A doorway is a perfect funnel. Only one person can come through it at a time. There may be a dozen of them trying to get at you, but you'll only have to deal with them one at a time.

Secondly, that doorway needs to be secured by a solid core door. In every modern home, interior doors are paper-thin hollow core. Any resolute kick can destroy them. And since most bedroom doors open inward, a stiff shoulder against the locked door will gain immediate access to your bedroom. This is not a good thing.

Thirdly, that solid-core door needs to be secured with a deadbolt lock. The bolt should extend at least one inch into the strike plate to assure that it will hold against a determined adversary. This also guarantees that the bolt will penetrate through the three-quarter-inch pine facing into the Douglas fir stud that composes most door jams. Now you have a lock that will hold until the entire door is destroyed.

Another useful locking tool is called a "door jammer." It's available at most hardware stores and consists of a metal pipe structure that fits securely under the doorknob and braces against your carpet or flooring, anchored by friction on its footplate. When an intruder presses against the door, the jammer is forced into more substantial contact with the floor. The harder he pushes, the more secure the jammer holds. A marvelous device, it's quick to install and quick to remove in case of emergencies. Another excellent use for a door jammer: it's very portable and will secure the door of a hotel or motel room. Are you confident and secure that the last occupant turned in their key?

To get through a dead-bolted solid-core door held in place by a jammer, the bad guy will have to chop the door to pieces to gain entry. How many bad guys are *THAT* determined? And if he does, what then?

The fourth step in fortifying your safe room is a firearm. This book is not a treatise on gunfighting tactics, but it is essential to discuss the practical choice and ramifications of using guns in a self-defense system.

A firearm is the tool of last resort in a self-defense system. The goal of this book is to *prevent* you from having to resort to a lethal force confrontation. By taking the commonsense practices advocated in this text, you will deter most everyone else. Still, there may be unusual times and situations when you must deal with a determined adversary who will not stop until he has killed you.

There is another benefit of choosing to use a firearm that is not usually discussed in self-defense texts. Having the resolve to use lethal force will fortify your mindset at earlier stages in the confrontation continuum. It predetermines that you are willing to take a life before you surrender your own. This adds real iron to your mindset that you will never give up—no matter what the cost to you or your adversary.

As stated before, the use of a firearm is a personal choice. According to a certain mindset found in tactical shooting classes, a firearm's purpose is to shoot holes in living things. Anything you do before that is merely practice for that eventuality.

The *ONLY* time a firearm is employed when there is a lethal force crisis--when you need to *SHOOT* somebody. It should NEVER be used as a bluff. Bad guys seem to know when you aren't a serious threat to their safety. That mindset isn't enough to deter a bad guy, let alone defeat him.

Perhaps you don't want to hurt the guy. Maybe you should only shoot to wound him? As civilized people, none of us want to kill somebody, do we?

Never shoot to wound!

Does that mean we shoot to kill? Not necessarily. Whether he lives or dies is NOT your concern. If you choose to use a firearm for personal defense, when the situation occurs, you must decide to shoot your attacker and continue shooting until the attack stops. As long as he continues attacking, you keep shooting. You don't determine whether he lives or dies—HE DOES. The sooner he stops attacking, the sooner you'll stop putting holes in him. It becomes another simple decision: when he stops—you stop.

Don't shoot to wound. Don't shoot to kill. *SHOOT TO LIVE!*

When you shoot somebody, the projectile will punch a hole through living tissue. Chances are, with a handgun, the adversary will survive. When he's hit, he will most likely run away (handguns are ballistically inferior to rifles and shotguns). Unlike what they show on TV, you will not be able to shoot the gun out of your adversary's hand. If you shoot him in the shoulder (a popular TV site for wounding), the bullet may penetrate through the deltoid muscle, bounce off his shoulder blade and ricochet through his heart and lungs. Or the bullet may sever the brachial artery. Either way, he will be dead before the paramedics arrive on the scene. And you just shot him in the shoulder!

If you choose to equip your safe room with a firearm, you must pre-make the decision that your life is worth defending, to the point that you will take another's life to do so. There must be no indecision at that critical point. Hunters have suffered "buck fever" where they have their sights aimed at their game and cannot take the shot. You can't afford to hesitate in a gunfight. As we stated in Condition Orange, pre-make the decision, establish your triggering event, and then stand ready to execute.

Not only is it critical that you pre-make the decision, but it is also just as essential that you commit to obtain the necessary training to assure that you will be competent in the use of your firearm. You will be held criminally responsible for knowing when it is legal to employ your gun. And you must be reasonably skilled in hitting your target.

According to available statistics from police records, the "three to five rule" applies to most gunfights. That means they happen within three to five yards, occur within three to five seconds, and exchange three to five rounds. They are brief, extremely close range, and exceedingly violent. As Colonel Cooper consistently emphasizes, your mindset will be much more critical than your accuracy.

Your shooting skills are still essential, mainly because they must be instinctive. Adding a major-league adrenaline dump adds to your difficulty coping, and your ability to manipulate the firearm will be significantly degraded, not to mention your accuracy.

Unlike the hit and miss drive-by shooters, we can't afford to have our rounds winging through the neighborhood. Massad Ayoob states it best when he claims: "You have a moral, legal, and financial responsibility for the terminal resting place of every projectile you fire." You can't afford to be negligent when involved in a gunfight. And there is nothing more negligent than a person who shoots a firearm at one person and accidentally hits another.

There is a higher level of responsibility when making a rational choice to shoot another human being. Ayoob makes an interesting point in his training tapes. As a private citizen in America, you are granted permission to take a human life in defense of your own (this is currently true as of this printing!). This independent decision is NOT allowed to any other single authority figure. No judge, no lawyer, no doctor can make this independent decision without juries, review boards, or family consent. As a private citizen, you have that Right, but along with it comes a higher level of responsibility.

The Right to take another's life in defense of your own is significantly limited to specific criteria. If you make a mistake while employing that Right, your actions can have "grave" consequences.

If you choose the responsibility to own and use a firearm for your defense, you must learn *when* to use it, *how* to use it, maintain it, and *store* it. Again, along with the Right comes a significant amount of responsibility.

Choosing a firearm is the last perimeter in your self-defense systems. It stands ready in the case that all of the other perimeters have not deterred your adversary. Chances are significantly higher that you will never have to resort to deadly force if you implement the other less-extreme elements.

Other safe room features that will assure the effectiveness of your barricade should include a cellular phone. Landlines can be cut or, if you have an extension phone in another room, the bad guys can disable your ability to call for help merely by taking it off "the hook."

So who do you call on your cell phone? Dialing 911 will get you to some general emergency number who will have to forward your call to your area's local law enforcement agency. That takes time, and time is the ally of the bad guys, not you. The more time they have, the more damage they're doing to your sound system, jewelry, or your safe room door. Much better: pre-program your cell phone to call the emergency number of your local police or sheriff. It shouldn't require any thought. You push a button, and presto: you're talking to a dispatcher.

Get a good quality flashlight. You don't necessarily need a five-cell baton to use as a short-range club. You may want something small that you can hold in your grip with your handgun. Just make sure the batteries are changed regularly, and it works! Murphy's Laws particularly apply to everything that runs on batteries.

Something the NRA astutely recommends is to have your front or backdoor keys attached to a glowstick. This will save you from the expense of replacing your front door.

When the police arrive, the first thing they will do is to establish a perimeter. How many units are required to secure the perimeter of *your* house? Most departments will require two, and some (especially corner homes) may require up to four cops to guarantee no more bad guys get in, and any bad guys coming out are suitably greeted. How long will it take for your local enforcement agency to get two to four cops at your home at two o'clock in the morning?

So while you're waiting, you'll be having a rather intense conversation with the dispatcher. Understand that the screen readout for the cell phone doesn't necessarily give the dispatcher enough information to send the necessary units. (Also, be aware that EVERYTHING YOU SAY IS BEING RECORDED!) So expect to have to provide a complete address, personal identification, and descriptions of yourself and your loved ones. Eventually, the cops will arrive.

It is critically important that you not race downstairs and greet the cops at the front door, especially with your firearm in your hand. You may be in your pajamas, but the police won't know you're the good guy. You'll have a lot of cops yelling at you with their guns pointed at you, especially if you're armed.

So stay in your safe room. Let the cops do the clearing of your house. How will they get in?

The police have a device called a ram. This heavy piece of pipe will not only break most locking mechanisms, but it will also take a lot of doors off their hinges. How much will it cost to replace your beautiful solid-core front door? No doubt several hundred dollars when you include the labor. A simple glow stick will save all that money.

When the police are on scene, tell the dispatcher that you will throw the key out the window to the scene's commanding officer. You have to identify which window you're nearest to so they can send the officer around to fetch the key. The chemical glow stick will be easy to see, even if you mess up your throw into those thorny rose bushes.

The dispatcher must identify the officer on the scene to you. Tossing your keys out into the dark to a waiting gang member won't help calm your adrenaline rush. Stay on the phone with the dispatcher until the police on the scene take charge of the situation.

By securing yourself in a suitably fortified safe room, you can prevent most every home defense lethal force situation. You won't have to deal with the adversary. You will probably suffer the theft of personal belongings and valuables, but you will be alive and healthy. If your belongings are valuable enough to the degree that you feel motivated to defend them, you can afford the insurance to replace them. Confident with your policy locked up there with you in your safe room, stay right there.

Lastly, home invasions have become a problem for many urban communities. You can prevent your home from being victimized by keeping your door locked and not opening it for anybody not personally acquainted with you. And be aware that anybody can get an official-looking ID badge. Any legitimate telephone repairman, gas or electric company person, or government official will understand why you insist on calling their department to verify their deployment before you allow them access. Another simple rule to add to your system is: don't open your door and won't be invaded.

CHAPTER 4

ALWAYS SAFE - CONCLUSION

Check-off lists are great. It eliminates memory as a pitfall. An old colloquialism is appropriate: "I trust a short pencil more than a long memory." Included at the end of this chapter is a check-off list to encourage you to survey and modify your home defense system's perimeters. Use it—harden your target.

On the street, there is no list. You must practice your defensive mindset and awareness until it becomes automatic as a state of mind. Cooper's alertness game is a good one. Mentally sizing up and silently discussing "what-if" situations will also keep your mind sharp and ready.

Develop and strengthen your "fighting mindset." Whenever you read about violent crime in the newspaper or see a crime story on television, personalize it. Use your imagination and walk yourself through it. Then make decisions about what YOU would do if confronted by that situation.

Make it as real and dangerous in your imagination as you can. If you can feel fear in your gut, then you're doing it right. If you're alone, go through the moves of evading your imaginary attacker. (Don't let people see you, or you'll feel stupid, and then you'll stop.)

Something Zen practitioners appreciate is that the brain cannot control the mind. You can order your brain not to think about the special dessert you want, but you know that thought, that image, that taste will be lingering there to torment you until you focus your mind on something more demanding. So we can't depend on our brain in a high-stress situation. We know that the logical, rational brain will not be available to help us due to the adrenaline dump. For self-defense purposes, we have to train the MIND, not the brain.

The way to affect the mind is by training the body. By performing any skill over a thousand repetitions, the body will learn the craft to be correctly performed. By performing the skill over a million times, it becomes automatic and unconscious. Bruce Lee said it best: "Conscious thought is the greatest hindrance to the proper execution of all physical action."

To be accomplished in any skill, all we have to do is practice. Some students become frustrated because they don't instantly grasp and obtain a particular skill immediately. The truth is we all learn at differing rates, but all of us can continue to learn and better ourselves with constant and unceasing practice.

Boxers "shadow box." They aren't just flailing about to show off. They are visually creating an opponent and seeing in their mind's eye as their adversary throws punches. And then they are training their bodies to react. By developing muscle memory, their counterpunches become instinctive. They won't SEE the openings in the guard of their opponent. They'll merely strike without conscious thought.

The more real you make it, your brain will recall these practiced reactions if or when a situation occurs. You see a robber approach with a gun; you'll instinctively run like the wind even before he can demand your money. You see a gang crossing the street to come at you; you'll immediately turn the other way and escape. You see the maddened ex-husband chopping through the safe room door with an ax; you won't hesitate to use your self-defense weapon.

The author Strong points out, your first best opportunity to stop a violent confrontation is in the first few seconds. If you immediately get away or get the upper hand, chances are the bad guy will stop and break off his attack. And if he doesn't stop, and your mindset is prepared to escalate as he does, you'll be one step ahead, ready to finish the fight that he started.

According to Strong:

> "With almost complete unison, sociologists and criminologists predict that, unless society makes drastic changes now, by the year 2005, we will experience another crime wave of unprecedented proportions."

Strong goes on to say that the future criminals are going to be more aggressive, more fearless, and more violent than at any time in our history.

We can't afford more police. Challenging the recommendations by Strong, we can't afford to give up more personal liberties. We certainly can't sit idly by and hope the police will be there to protect us from the onslaught. It's like a rancher loosing his dogs into the yard with a bunch of chickens and then punishing the dogs after they kill all the birds. We've got to stop being poultry.

There will always be those who will prey upon the weak. The best recourse is to strengthen ourselves to assure that we are NOT weak. Everybody doesn't need to enroll in karate and shooting schools (although it would considerably improve many of our current educational offerings!). But here's another excellent saying from my warrior friends: You can't truly call yourself "peaceful" unless you are capable of great violence. If you're not capable of violence, you're not peaceful; *you're harmless.*

What is vital is that each of us maintains our awareness to deter the simple street hood, the youthful gang banger, and the petty criminal. And the more prepared we are, the more resources we can deploy to deter a more dedicated adversary.

Lethal force is still a legal option in certain very specific situations. It is undoubtedly true, although politically incorrect to state that *deadly force solves recidivism.* A dead crook won't be committing another crime. Our moribund judicial system's revolving door slams shut when the bad guy is rerouted to the morgue.

We must make a life of crime short and dangerous. That has to be the primary goal of our personal safety. There are much smoke and mirrors in the political world, with elected officials touting their panacea of crime-solving laws---if we just surrender a little more of our freedom. There are so many political battles to be fought and so many social obstacles to be overcome that we may never flush the criminal sewage backing up on death row. As concerned citizens, we need to be involved with the electoral process to un-elect the Santa Claus judges and keep our police departments from becoming politicized. But it is on the street that we can have the most significant effect.

By adopting the proper mindset and following a few easy guidelines, we can make a difference and help our police stop crime. We must be pro-active in our self-defense and not become complacent. Like a disease organism, crime is always looking for a weakness, always looking for a victim to take over a feed upon. Our job is to remain steadfast in our vigil and remain…Always Safe.

HOME SECURITY CHECKLIST

Exterior

<u>Landscaping</u>: eliminate hiding places

- Use lighting and hostile plants where people can hide
- Trim hedges near windows and doors
- Trim trees to eliminate peeping toms

<u>Perimeter</u>

- Lock all doors and windows
- Don't hide keys outside

Interior

<u>Lighting</u>

- Night lights while you're home
- Activity lights (plus radio or TV) while you're away

Set things up to ensure that you never enter a darkened home.

Safe Room (a room that will secure everybody)

- One entrance with a dead bolt lock
- Phone (land line AND cell phone)
- Furniture placed to provide cover
- Self-defense implement
- Fire extinguisher
- Keys on a glow stick
- Sweats (for those who sleep in minimal clothing)